May Love Lead

Poetry for Living, Loving & Giving

Cheryl Lunar Wind and Friends

May Love Lead

Poetry for Living, Loving & Giving

Some of the poems in this collection first appeared in We Are One, We Are Light, We Are Forever and Creativity Brings Peace chapbooks; and on facebook.

Front cover photo credit, Amanda Lorence
Title inspiration, from A'Marie B. Thomas-Brown

First edition.
Published by Alexander Agency Books,
Mount Shasta, California 96067

ISBN 979-8-9897287-6-3

May Love Lead

Poetry for
Living, Loving & Giving

Dedicated
to Matthew, Cota, Dream Helper.
We love and appreciate you.
Fly Free!

"We are so lightly here.
It is in Love we are made.
In Love we disappear."
---Leonard Cohen

A Blessing from Pradeep Nawarathna

May you find wealth in the richness of a healthy mind.

Contentment as your treasure, true wealth as its kind.

May good health be your companion, in body and thought.

And unconditional love be the lesson you've been taught.

May the trust of friends surround you, like stars in the night---
Guiding your path with their steady, gentle light.

May you embrace freedom, unconditional and pure--
A bliss beyond compare, forever to endure.

In every breath, may wisdom be your guide, and in
your heart may compassion reside.

With every step, may peace be your way.

Blessings on your journey, each and every day!

Contents

Love Is 34
by Le'Vell Zimmerman

Contributors page

Author page & Testimonials

Welcome to Paradise
by Cody Ray Richardson

Come one come all
The gates are open
You yourselves hold the keys
All seen and un-seen
All guests and residents
No rituals required
No offerings needed
Acceptance and forgiveness
Are yours to converge
The son and daughter of creation and created
Allow yourself through...
You are welcomed to paradise with open arms
Forgiveness will allow you to unload your baggage
Acceptance will allow you to be as you are
A beautiful radiant eternal light being
I see you
I love you

Welcome... Welcome

(1144 6 8 2023)

How, Now, Wow
by Mikasa Tamara Blue Ray

Throw away the Past
Don't hold onto what doesn't Last
Just forget what Was
Don't live your life on Pause
That was Then
Don't get stuck in If and When
Now is Now
You don't need to know HOW
Because in every Now
Is the potential for that WOW
To Create with Trust
That will Always Last
To Restore that Trust in Yourself, You
Because You is the WHO
Yes YOU are The only ONE
Who can get your own job DONE
So don't from yourself Run
Instead have FUN
Own your emotional Wounds
You are not Doomed
You carry the greatest of Treasure
Within, if you turn it into Pleasure
Choose to step out of Victim Consciousness
Because you are neither "poor you" or Helpless
You are not LESS
Just CHOOSE aware and Create Happiness
Step out of the mind Neurosis
Don't listen to the Ego Diagnosis
Because YOU ARE, and within You know HOW
To turn it all around into the VICTORY of the NOW
Because you Are WORTHY and You DESERVE
Don't limit yourself, don't yourself Reserve
Choose to commit, the Divine Love SERVE
Because if you Through your Heart Observe
What has been within you Programmed
You will see it's a fake Hologram
Of who you THINK you Are
If you DEBUG this you will come Far
Life is more than having your own needs Met

2

Remember you can Create with Each Breath
So bravely choose the Ego Death
And transition into a New State of Mind
Where you are no longer Blind
In that Unity Consciousness you Will Find
How beautiful it is to BE, sharing and be Kind
Because you Are Self Love and feel LOVEABLE
Thus everything and all is POSSIBLE
You are the EXPANSION
Of CREATION
And know that with each NEW HEARTBEAT
You are fulfilled and COMPLETE
So you grab the Moment for a New Opportunity
In your Own Unity
To feel and be FULFILLED
And keep your DREAMLIFE Build
A NEW happier peaceful STORY
Because you no longer in the Past are Sorry
You Celebrate your Unique EXPRESSION
Freedom of Life lived in PASSION
You have regained the TRUST
And you don't have to anything Must
Life is simple, easy, you @JUST
Simply Because You TRUST
Knowing you are connected to the Creator FATHER
And the Weaving Creatrix MOTHER
Together with them you Can Create your Hearts Desires
But this Requires
Seeing and Loving Yourself into FREEDOM
As an amazing POWERFUL CREATOR Beacon

Green Light
by Le'Vell Zimmerman

Experience, then integration/implementation.

Receiving, then giving.

Rest, then action.

Acceptance, then contribution.

Feminine energy, then Masculine energy.

Within the Heart, then the Mind.

The cycles have a purpose beloved.

It's with great maturity that you work with these cycles of
life in allowing what you have to contribute/share with the
world to flourish beyond the impatience of your minds ambition.

When it's time, you will act.

It's with acceptance that you receive your "blueprints".

Only through more presence do you acknowledge these cycles.

The Divine Heart space will "give you the green light"
when it is time.

Do you trust yourself?

How much?

-3333

4

Mind & Body
by Pradeep Nawarathna

Mind and body, a duo so bright,
Dance through the day, rest in the night.
Thoughts like seeds, actions the fruit,
Together they play, in pursuit.

The mind tells tales, the body believes,
In this dance, who leads, who receives?
Healing and hurting, a balance so fine,
In the waltz of life, they align.

So let them dance, let them blend,
On this journey, from start to end.
Mind and body, in harmony,
Crafting life's rich tapestry.

There
by Cody Ray Richardson

There I sat
A place I had been several times before
A comfortable place
Where nature provides all that I need
For that I embrace it
I look forward to it
Normally when I'm there I think a lot
The more I think the less I see around me
The less nature is able to speak to me
The chatter in my mind severs the connection
The connection between the earth and I
The creature's seen and unseen
The beings felt and unfelt
So I diminish my thoughts
My feelings
I quiet my inner voice
I recognize it outside of this comforting connection
The more I focus on the comfort the more it embraces me
The more beauty I see
It washes me
It sets me free
Free from the loop
Free from the residue of social and technological interactions
There I remember why I am here
Why I am anywhere
Why I am
A servant
A guest
A student
A lucky soul
A happy person
Thank you nature
My friend
My lover
My mother
Thank you

Keep Living
by Cheryl

Be the light at the end of the tunnel.

Use your magic for good.

Be thankful for what you got.

You are an alchemist--
take a situation,
transmute it into
something
Better.

Own your gifts.
See clearly,
that you are gifted.

Ride the roller coaster.
Join the dance.
Be the conductor.

Play that funky music--
Shake your tail
Sail your boat
Spread your wings
Enter the art--
Gape. Vibe. Jive.

Name that tune.
Know your way.
Love your life.
Be the light!

Begin with Peace
by Pradeep Nawarathna

Be here now, in this moment's light,
Where worries fade and hearts take flight.
Accept the change, life's constant dance,
And in your patience, find romance.

Feel for others, in their shoes tread,
With kindness speak, let love be spread.
For what we have, give thanks and smile,
Less for ourselves, more for the mile.

In quiet thought, let wisdom grow,
And with each breath, let calmness flow.
When things can't change, just let them be,
In letting go, you will be free.

So take each step with gentle care,
In Buddha's way, find patience there.
With every breath, let peace flow in,
And with that peace, we all begin.

Release
by Pradeep Nawarathna

Letting go of wants, setting them free,
Opens the heart, lets us just be.
In the space where desires once spun,
Finds a calm mind, bright as the sun.

Happiness grows in this quiet place,
A gentle strength, a tender grace.
With each craving that we release,
Comes a greater sense of inner peace.

A smile, a curve that sets things straight,
Lifts the heart and lightens weight.
So smile a little, or maybe a lot,
And brighten the world with the joy you've got.

8

Little Things
by Pradeep Nawarathna

Happiness hides in little things,
In morning light, in bird that sings.

In every laugh, in love we share,
In winds of peace, in moments rare.

So take a breath, and let it be,
Find joy in life, in what you see.

In your own heart, the answer's found,
In simple love, where hope's unbound.

Intuition
by Pradeep Nawarathna

Your nerves, like strings, feel vibes around,
From those who lift you, to those who confound.
Trust this sense, it guides you true,
To people and places that resonate with you.

Will You Love Me?
by Ray El

Will you love me when I'm old?

Will you love me when it's cold?
Will you love me when I'm blue?
Will you love with love that's true?
Will you love me in the springtime?
Will you love me in the fall?
Will you love me in the nighttime?
Or will you love me not at all?
Will you love me?

I will love you every day!
I will love you in every way!
I will love you when you're sad!
I will love you, make you glad!
I will love you in the winter!
I will love you when it's hot!
I will love you in the daytime
With everything I've got!
I will love you!

We will love when we are old.
We will love when it is cold.
We will love when we are blue.
We will love with love so true.
We will love all year long.
We will love and sing our song.
We will share our love with others,
Our sisters and our brothers.
We will share God's Love and Light
Wherever we may go.
We will love!

I heard an angel whisper in my ear
by Ray El

I heard an angel whisper in my ear a fair and lovely tune
A song of hope and dreams, it was to lift me from gloom
She sang about love so dear for all of us on earth
From all those in heaven who see in us such worth
Let go of despair she sang, there's no reason to be sad
Lift up your hearts and feel God's love, be glad
He cares for each dear soul; He knows your every fear
Seek within your heart, He says, and find His Gift so dear
We all came to Earth, she sang, to turn this world around
To make the Earth a Heaven once more--Raise up this holy ground
Be joyful, she sang, be filled with hope, seek God's Will every day
He alone knows how to raise the Earth:
He'll show each one the way
When she had sung her song, returned to Heaven,
a solemn vow I swore
To know His Will, to spread His Love,
that Earth may rise once more!

Recipe for Abundance
by Pradeep Nawarathna

In the sacred garden of existence, we stand,
Where energies weave and blessings expand.
May abundance flow like a gentle stream,
Nourishing every dream, every heartfelt scheme.

❄ *Earth's Bounty*
From the fertile soil, roots dig deep,
Drawing sustenance, secrets they keep.
May your endeavors bear fruits untold,
Harvests of plenty, a life manifold.

✹ *Celestial Alignment*
Look to the stars, their cosmic dance,
Planets whisper secrets, in a celestial trance.
May Jupiter's largesse, Venus's grace,
Guide you toward abundance's embrace.

🔥 *Inner Fire*
Within your core, a sacred flame,
Igniting passions, dreams aflame.
May it burn bright, fueling your quest,
For wealth of spirit, and treasures best.

♦ *Golden Threads*
Imagine threads of gold, weaving fate,
Connecting you to destiny's gate.
May opportunities shimmer, paths unfold,
Riches of heart, and fortunes untold.

❀ *Lotus Blooms*
Visualize a lotus, petals unfurl,
Emerging from mud, a radiant swirl.
May your life bloom, each petal a gift,
Abundance in love, joy, and uplift.

🌊 *Ocean's Tides*
Picture waves, ebbing and flowing,
Tides of fortune, their rhythm knowing.
May prosperity surge, like ocean's kiss,
Filling your sails with abundance's bliss.

🌈 *Rainbow's Promise*
After the storm, behold the arc,
A rainbow bridge, where blessings embark.
May its colors paint your days anew,
Abundance in every shade, every hue.

🎭 *Gratitude's Key*
Unlock abundance with gratitude's key,
For what you receive, what you see.
May thankfulness open doors wide,
Inviting prosperity to forever abide.

**May abundance be your birthright, dear soul,
In wealth of love, purpose, and self-made whole.
As you journey, may blessings cascade,
Abundance in every step, every serenade.**

Walking the Way of Wisdom
by Cheryl

Detach---
Be the observer.

Be like the White Knight---
he walks in kindness and compassion.

Compassion
is purity in action.

See the beauty in all perspectives.

Expect a view
that is different than yours.

Be open to New Ways
of doing, thinking, expressing---

We are beautiful in our uniqueness.
Appreciate that variety.

Allow Free Will
the space
to expand.

Reality by Cheryl

Handle each situation with finesse--

Trust that wisdom will guide you.

Enter new territory with awe.

Expansion requires patience.

Your victory will be epic.

We'll all be the winners.

Your actions are your reality.

14

Radio Receiver
by Le'Vell Zimmerman

The "thoughts" don't belong to you beloved.

You are the observer here beyond this constant mental activity.

The true self is not "thinking anything"...

Who you are as a conscious being has the ability to "select" the ideas and thought patterns you emotionally entertain, however the ideas as simply frequencies that are present in your immediate energetic environment.

The human brain operates as a "radio receiver" constantly translating these frequencies as ideas and/or "talking/dialogue" you perceive mentally that have nothing to do with you as the silence observing this dialogue as an expression of The Creator.

The talking in your head is not
"your consciousness",
but the lower frequency programming
most of this species has become accustomed
to voicing.

Healing is a free will choice indeed.

-4444

Transmission From Owl
by Sabinananda Ananda

Love Is clear Seeing -
through the Eyes of the heart.
Ask yourself,
Who,
Who,
Who...
Who sees?
If there is any sense of owning this heart seeing,
then it is not love,
then it is perceiving
through the personal,
and therefore
limited,
lens.
Set the perceiving free.
Who sees?
Love sees.
Who loves?
Love loves.
That is love.
Set love Free.
Simply Being Love
witnessing ItSelf.

The One
by Le'vell Zimmerman

Many will say that this incarnation is like "a game",
however the great suffering and destruction you
observe that many are experiencing at present
here in the physical is "absolutely nothing to play with".

There are no "winners or losers" here either, where
such a path has its foundation within you in being
a hologram involving you observing reflections of
yourself as The One, where the premise is the
expansion of your capacity of acceptance of yourself...

Unconditionally.

As God, you are not here to "play anybodies games"
beloved.

Being "serious" is about being at peace, in
objective observation and consideration of your
own Light beyond the personalization of your
conscious present in the physical.

This is about who you are as God.

Love is "the fabric"...

Peace is its eternal frequency.

Breathe beloved.

-5555

Your Liberation
by Le'Vell Zimmerman

The less pressure, the more freedom.

The more freedom, the more creativity.

The more creativity, the more Divinity.

Small steps back to Heaven.

Only you can liberate yourself beloved.

No one is here "to save you".

That's your job.

Let's go God.

-333

Creation is with you
by Cody Ray Richardson

In the frequency of love

There is only limitless expansion

Focus on what you want

Are you trading the future for the past

Let it go nothing lasts

Life is all that you attract

With thought alone all is born

Confrontation an opportunity

For a new you to be born

Creation is with you

You are never alone

It's Gonna Get Done
by Cheryl

How do we practice acceptance?

By knowing that all is happening
according to divine plan--

for soul growth--
We signed up for this.

Resistance is futile,
more than that
it's harmful.

So--
might as well
just
Go with the flow.

Live & Let Live

The symphony that prime creator wrote--
is Divine Will.

We all have a part to play
in the Divine Symphony.

There will be an end,
and it will be glorious!

It's gonna get done.

"Live and Let Live" is an expression that will allow for more alignment, harmony, and grace during this transition amongst your brothers and sisters, where magical nature of integrating with your Higher Self in the physical is birthing a Galactic presence within you that is truly "The Return of Christ" in a manner that the Multiverse has never seen before.
---Le'Vell Zimmerman

Failure Will Be My Pillow
by Cody Ray Richardson

I'm letting it all fall away
The plan
The possessions
The group
I've given too much
I will no longer trade the past for the future
Pain for pleasure
Providing for love
What's meant for me
Will come to me
I give up completely
All goes out the window
Failure will be my pillow
Nature will take care of me
Nature never lies
Never manipulates
Never tries
It's time I learn to listen
Like nature does to me
I am awake
I am tired from living a dream

Gentle Strength *
by Cheryl

horses, running,
hair blowing---
golden,
wheat swaying
gently.

The gently moving tree
does not break
in the storm
because she is flexible,
willing to bend.

Do not
Be rigid
in your ways---
soften your thoughts
and your feelings will flow
free
like fast waters.

Go
Gently,
down the stream.

*Title inspiration from Jennifer H.

Water, water on the fall
by Cody Ray Richardson

Infinite messages
Timeless collection of ancient language
It passes through me every day
I see it for what I see
Oh so much I wish I didn't miss
Memories embedded
Sacred songs
Every rudiment within
Every pattern
Every conversation
A movie of what was
Some of what will be
Some a reflection
Water, water on the fall
You are the most wonderful of us all
Your consistent pattern
Yet ever changing
Following laws set
Providing for all
Leaving none for yourself
A true servant
True shape shifter
All your forms of alchemy
In your presence
My mind is free
My heart is open
To possibility
Water, water on the fall
Love us
Nourish us
Bless us all

Heart of Eternity
by Mikasa Tamara Blue Ray

This is The Golden Dance
Of True Sacred Romance
Their Soul plays the Greatest of Love Song
About their Hearts being so brave and Strong
Waiting for lifetimes to meet once Again
But the wait was never in Vain
Because beyond Earthly Reality
Lives their Love in the Higher Heart of Eternity
There their Love forever Remains
Pulsating in their Holy Veins
Within their Union Peaceful Stillness Reigns
Happiness and Joy Gains
Ahh, such a Sacred Space
Their Soulful Revelations of Each other
Interlace
Building Hearth of Warming Flames
Crossing Multidimensional Planes
/Mika Sa Ta MaRa

Grandmother Pine
by Cheryl

So much gratitude
for sunlight on
green pine needles
long, an elder tree--
like the deer who
carries a large rack
on his head.

The sky and tree branches
combine in a kaleidoscope
fashion-- small shapes
of blue peeking thru.

The huge pinecones represent new life.

The plants inside are
reaching thru the blinds
to touch her--
like hands on the glass prison window
separating loved ones from each other.

I can't believe they took the
life of her brother,
across the parking lot
where I live---
his pieces lay in a pile
in the neighbor's carport.

The power company--
like taking children away from
their families to 'educate'
them, because it was deemed
appropriate.

The arrogance of this country
and culture-- that I am a dweller of.

The patience of Grandmother Pine--
she tells me the new way is coming--
My dear heart, do not allow
discouragement to take hold.

Mudra Meditation
by Yvonne Trafton

Sunflower bloom smilings
Mudra humble meditation
greeted upon laughter from outside
Outside, laughters tears flow~
mudra humble meditations
oh, humble mudras
Iam so humbled, so humbled
Humbled by you 'all'
'all' of you "in sitting"
sitting with you in circle--
Sitting in Grace.
In grace sitting.
Radiance of grace.
Humbled by who came,
humbled by High Ones
sitting in circle with 'All' High Selves
humbling, humbling
mudra of self
self in mudra
Buddha sits before me in mudra
Giant mala beads glow
Lighted Buddha.
Prays to me.
Rejoice for me.
Crows sing.
Temple doors seal.
My temple doors sing.
Jesus bare chested kneels beside me
he rests on my lap
arms head rest
backs' fresh whip marks
Jesus looks me in the eyes
Heart mudra, heart mudra
Kwan Yin's mudra pose
Heart Lotus Mudra
she glows before me
In hour-glass pose
Hour-glass mudra
fill your sands below
fill your sands above

fill your heart sands
heart fillings of joy gatherings
joy gatherings, joy gatherings
humbled before her--
Humbled before me
joyful gatherings
Spirit fillings
My High Self in sitting pose
giant lotus in my lap
Blossoming Lotus opens
Birthing Lotus Iam
Large red mirror "master crystal" cathedral
on fire, red a-glow
red crystal energy feedings of
blooming Lotus
My lotus a-lite, a-lite Iam
Joyful humble gatherings
Joy for who 'came'
Joy for you who 'come'
Joy for 'me'
Me in joy.

MY Head bowed in prayer mudra
Hands in prayer.
My Eagle wings
Have come out.
Eagle wings spread,
Wings flapping.
Iam Eagle flying.
Eagle mudras.
Iam of "golden" Light Eagle
Iam so humbled
Humble Mudras!

~AHO~
Yvonne Trafton
Golden Eagle

Let Grace Flow
by Pradeep Nawarathna

In the quietude of sacred breath,

Where lotus petals unfurl upon still waters,

We find the grace that dances between realms.

Listen, dear traveler, to the sutras whispered by the wind:

"Amazing grace! (how sweet the sound!)
That saved a wretch like me!"

Within the tapestry of existence, threads intertwine:

Silk spun from joy, shadows cast by sorrow.

The Buddha's gaze, compassionate and unwavering,

Rests upon your weary heart.

Let grace flow, a gentle stream through ancient groves.

Each step, a prayer etched in sandstone.

As the sun kisses the horizon,

May your wounds find solace in the moon's embrace.

You are not alone.

The Bodhisattvas, luminous and tender,

Walk beside you, their footsteps echoing in temple halls.

Inhale the fragrance of incense,

Exhale the weight of countless lifetimes.

Know this:

Your suffering is but a dewdrop on a spider's silk.

Grace, like morning mist, envelops all.

When the world trembles,

When the heart quivers,

Remember:

You are stardust and moonbeams,

Whispers of eternity.

May your journey be a pilgrimage of awakening.

May your wounds bloom into lotus blossoms.

And when the final stanza is sung,

May grace cradle you,

As the river meets the sea.

Love Is
by Jennifer H.

Love is freedom
never pushing over me
only holding me steady,
as I tread these murky waters.
Gently lifting me when I feel down

Slowly caressing the fear and pain
till it loosens it's grip and leaves
my body

Love is Pure never telling me who to be
only showing me what I can be,
and how to get there

Love never pulls or pushes me
wanting me to feel low
to the ground

Love builds me up, wanting
me to be, all that I can be

Guiding me forward
shining a light so bright
all that is not right
for me dissolves away

May Love Lead
by A'Marie B. Thomas-Brown

Waking up from a long sleep
The wind
The whales
The birds
The trees
Such glee as I am remembering
Your laughter and humor
To be awakened from slumbering stupor
To see what living is for
Hiding the light no more
As ignorance is not bliss
I stand face to face
And we kiss
Love intertwines in the words, the spaces,
the diction
As we listen to the sound
As Light
We ride
The tide
Ocean to Ocean
Moment by Moment
Beyond breath
With nothing left I wept

May Love Lead
Spirit keep
And we breathe
As One

Trust Love by Cheryl

trust love,
she'll show the way

no more confusion, competition, doubt--

At the end of the day,
the only choice
is between love and fear.

The sun will set,
and all is well.

Look to the Sky

by Pradeep Nawarathna

See the stars, their silent glow,
Goals like constellations, they show.
Obstacles fade, like shadows at dawn,
Positive thoughts, a universe reborn.

Embrace beauty, like petals unfurl,
Clear the mind, let negativity swirl.
Stay on track, a comet's bright flight,
Humanity's grace, in the cosmic night.

Truth is Simple

by Le'Vell Zimmerman

The truth can be extremely simple beloved.
Simplicity allows for it to function eternally.
And so it is with all Universal Laws.
-333

Love Is

by Le'Vell Zimmerman

Yes, embrace your preferences, however to remain balanced beyond rejection or resentment is where you embody the purity of your essence.

In truth, all must do what they need to, to heal.

If you want to help, heal yourself through self acceptance and allow all to see beyond any expectations.

This is the greatest service you can provide all life beloved.

Masters know.

Gratitude.

-333

Many thanks to these contributors:

Sabinananda Ananda

Ray El

Jennifer H.

Pradeep Nawarathna (pcnawarathna@gmail.com)

Mikasa Tamara Blue Ray

Cody Ray Richardson

A'Marie B. Thomas-Brown

Yvonne Trafton

Le'Vell Zimmerman

Author page--

Cheryl Lunar Wind lives in the Mount Shasta area in a little town called Weed. She is a practicer of Mayan cosmology, Lakota ceremony, Star Knowledge and the Universal Laws including the Law of One. Her hobbies are writing poetry, music, dance, drum circles and love for all life; plant, animal and crystal. Cheryl has been a guide and spiritual teacher for many years. Now she shares wit and wisdom through poetry, and has published poetry books; Know Your Way, We Are One, Follow the White Rabbit, Love Your Light, LIFE: Shared thru Poetry, Come to Mount Shasta: Sacred Path Poetry, We Are Light, Finding Our Way Home, We Are Forever, Handshake With the Divine, Grand Rising: A New Day Has Dawned, Star Messages: Codes to Sing, Dance and Live by, Return to Innocence, Bloom Like Nature: Live the Natural Way, Creativity Brings Peace: Create & Share Your Gifts and May Love Lead: Poetry for Living, Loving & Giving.

Testimonials---

"Cheryl's poetry is very inspiring--particularly the way she compares life with the forces of nature. There is a special element in her poems that opens my heart and fills my soul with divine possiblities."
Giovanna Taormina, Co-Founder, One Circle Foundation

"Cheryl's poems have helped me to uncover and honor my own hidden memories. The beauty of her spirit is evident in each tender, insightful passage."
Marguerite Lorimer, www.earthalive.com

"A rare collection filled with raw, courageous honesty. Thought provoking words that will stop you in your tracks."
Snow Thorner, ED Open Sky Gallery, Montague, California

"When wisdom, guidance, confirming comfort, ect. arrives to us humans--from beings with the perspective of other realms--it is a divine gift. Especially in the form of what we call poetry, and through a being with no agenda;

Cheryl Lunar Wind simply shares what source gives her!"
---Dragon Love (Thomas) Budde

Cheryl,
Greetings and Happy Monday to you my friend. I just
wanted to share with you that every time I read
'Come to Mount Shasta', even now that I'm mentioning
it I cry, I cannot help it, it is such a Divine message and
so impeccable in its timing. I came up here for Spirit, you
know I was called by Source and I live on the mountain
and I just want to thank you. Your poem found me last
summer at the headwaters during the Alien and Angels
conference; and then I found your book sitting in the
gazebo and I just can't stop, I love it! I love you, thank you.
---Jim

Cheryl,
Just want to thank you for your bringing me into the community
at Shasta. What you are doing/did do is absolutely changing
my life. You did it, you were instrumental in helping me set
my true path. Spirit is moving and the more of us that listen
and act the sooner the shift will be completed.
---Darrel

About Cheryl's poetry--
"You are dynamic! I have known no one who does so much so
swiftly, and your writing touches my heart because it comes
from your heart."
---The Durwood Show

"Your words are my words. I keep your book 'Know Your Way'
on my nightstand. I read it at bedtime and morning."
---Karina Arroyo

"Cheryl's words work magic in my heart, stirring the wisdom
that is buried so deeply within me---beautiful indeed!"
---Ellie Pfeiffer, founder of Ellie's Espresso & Bakery, Weed, CA